The
Love Poems
of John Keats

John Keats

The
Love Poems
of John Keats

In Praise of Beauty

*Selected and with an
Introduction by
David Stanford Burr*

St. Martin's Press
New York

THE LOVE POEMS OF JOHN KEATS: IN PRAISE OF BEAUTY. Copyright © 1990
by St. Martin's Press, Incorporated. Introduction Copyright © 1990 by
David Stanford Burr. All rights reserved. Printed in China.
No part of this book may be used or reproduced in any manner
whatsoever without written permission except in the case of brief quota-
tions embodied in critical articles or reviews. For information, address
St. Martin's Press, 175 Fifth Avenue, New York, N.Y. 10010.

www. stmartins.com

Production Editor: David Stanford Burr

Design by Glen M. Edelstein

Library of Congress Cataloging-in-Publication Data

Keats, John, 1795–1821.
   The love poems of John Keats : in praise of beauty / John Keats.
     p. cm.

  ISBN 13: 978-0-312-05105-1
  ISBN 10: 0-312-05105-0

  1. Love poetry, English. I. Title.
PR4832 1990
821'.7—dc20   90-36880
                 CIP

11 12 13

Contents

Introduction vii

"Fill for me a brimming bowl" 1
To Some Ladies 3
To Emma 5
"Woman! when I behold thee flippant, vain" 6
To [Mary Frogley] 9
To ——— 12
To a Young Lady who sent me a Laurel Crown 13
Lines 15
Stanzas 16
"Hither, hither, love—" 18
"Think not of it, sweet one, so—" 21
"In drear-nighted December" 22
"When I have fears that I may cease to be" 24
"O Blush not so! O blush not so!" 26
To ——— 28
"Where be ye going, you Devon maid?" 29
"Over the hill and over the dale" 30
"And what is love? It is a doll dressed up" 32
Song 33
The Eve of St. Agnes 35
La Belle Dame sans Merci. A Ballad 51
"The day is gone, and all its sweets are gone!" 54
"What can I do to drive away" 56
"I cry your mercy, pity, love—ay, love!" 58
"Bright star! would I were steadfast as thou art—" 59
To Fanny 61

Introduction

John Keats was born on October 31, 1795, in London, the eldest child of Thomas and Frances Keats. Thomas, a prosperous livery stable keeper, died on April 16, 1804, after a fall from a horse; Frances remarried two months later, leaving the Keats children, George, Tom, and Fanny—another brother, Edward, died in infancy from tuberculosis—to live with their grandparents. In June their grandfather died and about five years later, shortly after her brother's death from tuberculosis, alcoholic and tubercular Frances returned to live with her mother and the children. Fourteen-year-old John nursed his mother through the last stages of illness until her death in March 1810. The three surviving male children would also succumb to tuberculosis: Tom at nineteen years, John at twenty-five, and George at forty-four.

John entered the progressive Clarke boarding school in 1803, where he gained more of a reputation as a fighter than a scholar; however, he dedicated himself to intense reading and voluntary work and won a book prize for a translation of the *Aeneid*. At fifteen, John left school and began an apprenticeship to Thomas Hammond as an apothecary-surgeon, and after a year's training at Guy's Hospital in London he qualified to practice medicine. Keats continued his literary studies with the encouragement of Charles Cowden Clarke, the headmaster's son from his old school, and wrote his first poetry when he was eighteen. He decided to forsake a medical career to pursue poetry, a choice scorned by Richard Abbey, the tightfisted guardian and trustee of the Keats children who was chosen by their grandmother before her death in 1814. Keats was accepted into the literary circle of politically liberal Leigh Hunt, who nicknamed him "Junkets" and published his fine sonnet "On First Looking into Chapman's Homer" in 1816.

Keats attended lectures by the well-known critic William Hazlitt, enjoyed the social milieu of artists and writers in London (including Shelley), and met with Wordsworth.

Poems, Keats's first volume of poems, published on March 3, 1817, was not well received by the public, and in April he began passionately reading Shakespeare and composing *Endymion*. *Endymion* is an allegory of imagination in pursuit of ideal beauty that ends with the mortal shepherd, Endymion, achieving apotheosis and union with the goddess Cynthia. Keats believed that great poets should write epic-length poems, and *Endymion*'s four thousand lines served as a maturing exercise toward his literary aspiration. In "Isabella; or, the Pot of Basil" (written February-April 1818), Lorenzo, the lover of Isabella, is murdered by her two brothers. Isabella discovers the buried body, cuts off the head, and keeps it in a pot of basil that she waters with her tears until the brothers steal the pot, discover its contents, and flee. Isabella, devastated by the double loss of Lorenzo, dies. In April 1818 *Endymion*—with its memorable first line, "A thing of beauty is a joy forever"—was published to hostile reviews that stopped sales: Keats's poem was an easy target for Tory reviewers who wished to attack Leigh Hunt. In June, Keats bid good-bye to George Keats and his bride, Georgiana, who sailed for America, and then he and his friend, Charles Brown, undertook a walking tour of the Lake District and Scotland that John had to cut short due to a severe sore throat. When John returned, he nursed his brother, Tom, whose tuberculosis had worsened. In spite of John's efforts Tom died on December 1, 1818, fueling John's premonition about his own death.

After Tom's death John went to live with Charles Brown at Wentworth Place in Hampstead, which had been rented during the summer by the widowed Mrs. Brawne, who had a son and two daughters. Keats had met the eighteen-year-old Fanny Brawne in November of 1818 and soon fell in love with her. He and Fanny seem to have reached an informal engagement on Christmas Day; however, Keats's finances and developing poor health would prevent any formal announcement of their engagement. In April, the Brawnes returned to Wentworth, and John and Fanny, now neighbors separated only by a wall, could see each other regularly. In January of 1819, inspired with love for Fanny, Keats wrote "The Eve of St. Agnes," an enchanting fairy-tale romance in Spenserian stanzas. The poem grew out of a popular superstition that a virgin who fasts and observes the rites of St. Agnes' eve (January 20) will see her lover in a dream that night. This romance of wish-fulfillment, full of sensuous imagery and medieval resonance, has been cited as the most beautiful short narrative in English poetry. The incomplete poem, "The Eve of St. Mark," followed, and, on April 21, 1819, Keats wrote "La Belle Dame sans Merci. A Ballad," which mysteriously hints at the spell that a supernatural, merciless, and fatal lady casts on a hapless knight-at-arms. Then, in the spring of 1819, Keats wrote four of his great odes: "Ode to Psyche," "Ode to a Nightingale," "Ode on a Grecian Urn," and "Ode to Melancholy."

Keats referred to his passionate love for Fanny as both a "pleasure and a torment." He wished for her love above all else, but feared that "being settled in the world" would stifle his growth as a poet. He could not write when in proximity to her and spent the summer of 1819 on the Isle of Wight, where he composed *Lamia*, a narrative in pentameter couplets. In the poem, Lycius falls in love with Lamia, a beautiful serpent-woman, who creates an illusory world that surrounds the lovers. The philosopher Appolonius divines Lamia's nature and denounces her, which causes her disappearance and Lycius' death. Keats's collaboration with Charles Brown on the dramatic tragedy *Otho the Great* was left incomplete, as was his reworking of the earlier *Hyperion. A Fragment* (written August-December 1818) into *The Fall of Hyperion. A Dream*. In September 1819 he composed the fifth great ode, "To Autumn," and returned to London where he wrote four scenes of *King Stephen*, a tragedy that would not be finished. He also began a satire, *The Jealousies (The Cap and Bells)*, which also would not be completed.

In October the symptoms of the family disease reappeared, and on February 3, 1820, John suffered a hemorrhage that he recognized as his "death-warrant." Later in March, Fanny refused his offer to end their engagement. After another hemorrhage in June, he moved back to Wentworth Place to be nursed by Fanny and Mrs. Brawne. The tuberculosis aggravated his unreasonable fits of jealousy and possessiveness toward Fanny. He thought she loved him less than he loved her, that she would find someone else to love.

Lamia, Isabella, The Eve of St. Agnes and Other Poems, his third collection, came out in July. This final collection, which contained the famous odes, received favorable reviews, but John, now much weakened, was forced to sail for Italy on September 18, 1820, to avoid the English winter. The young painter, Joseph Severn, accompanied Keats to Rome, nursed him during the final months, and held him in his arms when he died on February 23, 1821. John Keats was buried in the Protestant cemetery in Rome—Shelley, another of the great Romantic poets, was to join him there a little over a year later. Keats requested that his tombstone bear the inscription: Here lies one whose name was writ on water.

Keats's letters chronicle the three years of his greatest productivity prior to the last year and a half when he was unable to write verse. It is clear that he wanted the letters preserved. Perhaps he felt they would contribute to his ambition of leaving behind some "immortal work" by which he would be remembered. Indeed, this epistolary legacy is considered to be the most famous collection of love letters in the English language. Keats's ardent professions of love for Fanny and his poignant entreaties for her to love him more, as he lay helpless and dying, offer an endearing glimpse into a very human and tormented soul. He wrote Fanny: "I have two luxuries to brood over . . . your Loveliness and the hour of my death," and "Love is my religion—I could die for that. I would die for you. My Creed is Love and you are its only tenet." In his last letter to Mrs. Brawne on October 24, 1820, Keats ends his thoughts with: "Good bye Fanny! God bless you."

substituted Georgiana's name for Emma's. The three Petrarchan sonnets that comprise "Woman! when I behold thee flippant, vain" (written before December 1815) shows Keats's indebtedness to Edmund Spenser's *The Faerie Queene*. Calidore, the Red Cross Knight, and Leander are legendary examples of devoted lovers. Keats is reported to have wept when he penned the "milk-white lamb" section, swept away by the tenderness of his imagination. "To [Mary Frogley]" (February 14, 1816) was a valentine that originally had been written for George to send to a cousin, Mary Frogley. Another valentine written on the same date, "To———" seems to hint at Keats's dissatisfaction with his five-foot-and-three-quarter-inch height. "To a Young Lady who sent me a Laurel Crown" (October-November 1816) probably was addressed to Georgiana, who sympathized with John's desire to forego medicine for poetry and who also cheered him after Mr. Abbey's discouraging reaction to John's literary declaration. "Lines" (before April 17, 1817) contains an instance of Keats's usage of sexual slang in the line "I'll feel my heaven anew." "Stanzas" is chronologically grouped with the preceding and succeeding poem. The last stanza of "Hither, hither, love—" recalls lines in Keats's letters addressed to Fanny Brawne. "Think not of it, sweet one, so—" (about November 11, 1817) was a song written for the entertainment of two cousins, Jane and Marianne Reynolds. "In drear-nighted December" (December 1817) contains elements of Keats's philosophy of Negative Capability in the line, "The feel of not to feel it." "When I have fears that I may cease to be" (January 22–31, 1818) demonstrates Keats's growing preference for the Shakespearean over the Petrarchan sonnet pattern and owes its inspiration to that "fair creature" in the Vauxhall Gardens in the summer of 1814. "O blush not so! O blush not so!" (January 31, 1818) is an amusing song full of sexual puns. "To———" (February 4, 1818) is a Shakespearean sonnet dedicated to the unknown Vauxhall lady. "Where be ye going, you Devon maid?" (about March 21, 1818) with its sexual innuendo and the bawdy "Over the hill and over the dale" (about March 23, 1818) are both songs; the latter celebrates Keats's visit to the Easter fair at Dawlish—*Venus* was the colloquial designation for prostitute. "And what is love? It is a doll dressed up" (conjectural, 1818) contains a reference to Cleopatra, who was said to have dissolved and drunk a pearl. "Song" (December 1818) was composed to accompany a Spanish air that Charlotte Reynolds used to play for Keats. "The Eve of St. Agnes" (January 18-February 2, 1819) is a metrical romance in the Spenserian mode, the first poem inspired by Fanny Brawne. "La Belle Dame sans Merci. A Ballad" (April 21, 1819) has the same title as that of the Provençal ditty Porphyro sings to Madeline in "The Eve of St. Agnes." "The day is gone, and all its sweets are gone!" (about October 10, 1819) is another Shakespearean sonnet, and "What can I do to drive away" (about October 13, 1819) is an irregular ode reflecting Keats's contradictory feelings about Fanny Brawne. "I cry your mercy, pity, love—ay, love!" (about October 1819) is a sonnet that voices Keats's fear of Fanny's inconstancy. "Bright star! would I were steadfast as thou art—" (conjectural, 1819), another Shakespearean sonnet, contains the recurring Keatsian theme of early death. "To Fanny" (February 1820) is an ode written shortly after the "death-warrant" hemorrhage and his subsequent indoor confinement.

—David Stanford Burr
New York City
March 1990

The
Love Poems
of John Keats

"Fill for me a brimming bowl"

What wondrous beauty! From this
moment I efface from my mind all
women.

> —Terence, *Eunuch* II.3.296

Fill for me a brimming bowl
And let me in it drown my soul:
But put therein some drug, designed
To banish Woman from my mind:
For I want not the stream inspiring
That heats the sense with lewd desiring,
But I want as deep a draught
As e'er from Lethe's waves was quaffed;
From my despairing breast to charm
The Image of the fairest form
That e'er my revelling eyes beheld,
That e'er my wandering fancy spelled.

'Tis vain! away I cannot chase
The melting softness of that face,
The beaminess of those bright eyes,
That breast—earth's only Paradise.

My sight will never more be blessed;
For all I see has lost its zest:

Nor with delight can I explore
The Classic page, the Muse's lore.

Had she but known how beat my heart,
And with one smile relieved its smart,
I should have felt a sweet relief,
I should have felt "the joy of grief."
Yet as a Tuscan 'mid the snow
Of Lapland thinks on sweet Arno,
Even so for ever shall she be
The Halo of my Memory.

To Some Ladies

What though, while the wonders of nature exploring,
  I cannot your light, mazy footsteps attend;
Nor listen to accents that, almost adoring,
  Bless Cynthia's face, the enthusiast's friend:

Yet over the steep, whence the mountain stream rushes,
  With you, kindest friends, in idea I muse—
Mark the clear tumbling crystal, its passionate gushes,
  Its spray that the wild flower kindly bedews.

Why linger you so, the wild labyrinth strolling?
  Why breathless, unable your bliss to declare?
Ah! you list to the nightingale's tender condoling,
  Responsive to sylphs, in the moon-beamy air.

'Tis morn, and the flowers with dew are yet drooping,
  I see you are treading the verge of the sea:
And now! ah, I see it—you just now are stooping
  To pick up the keep-sake intended for me.

If a cherub, on pinions of silver descending,
  Had brought me a gem from the fret-work of heaven;
And, smiles with his star-cheering voice sweetly blending,
  The blessing of Tighe had melodiously given;

It had not created a warmer emotion
  Than the present, fair nymphs, I was blessed with from you,

Than the shell, from the bright golden sands of the ocean
   Which the emerald waves at your feet gladly threw.

For, indeed, 'tis a sweet and peculiar pleasure
   (And blissful is he who such happiness finds),
To possess but a span of the hour of leisure,
   In elegant, pure, and aërial minds.

To Emma

Oh come, dearest Emma! the rose is full blown,
And the riches of Flora are lavishly strown,
The air is all softness, and crystal the streams,
And the West is resplendently clothèd in beams.

We will hasten, my fair, to the opening glades,
The quaintly carved seats, and the freshening shades,
Where the faeries are chanting their evening hymns,
And in the last sunbeam the sylph lightly swims.

And when thou art weary I'll find thee a bed
Of mosses and flowers to pillow thy head;
There, beauteous Emma, I'll sit at thy feet,
While my story of love I enraptured repeat.

So fondly I'll breathe, and so softly I'll sigh,
Thou wilt think that some amorous Zephyr is nigh—
Ah, no!—as I breathe, I will press thy fair knee,
And then thou wilt know that the sigh comes from me.

Then why, lovely girl, should we lose all these blisses?
That mortal's a fool who such happiness misses.
So smile acquiescence, and give me thy hand,
With love-looking eyes, and with voice sweetly bland.

"Woman! when I behold thee flippant, vain"

Woman! when I behold thee flippant, vain,
   Inconstant, childish, proud, and full of fancies;
   Without that modest softening that enhances
The downcast eye, repentant of the pain
That its mild light creates to heal again:
   E'en then, elate, my spirit leaps, and prances,
   E'en then my soul with exultation dances
For that to love, so long, I've dormant lain:
But when I see thee meek, and kind, and tender,
   Heavens! how desperately do I adore
Thy winning graces;—to be thy defender
   I hotly burn—to be a Calidore—
A very Red Cross Knight—a stout Leander—
   Might I be loved by thee like these of yore.

Light feet, dark violet eyes, and parted hair,
   Soft dimpled hands, white neck, and creamy breast,
   Are things on which the dazzled senses rest
Till the fond, fixèd eyes, forget they stare.
From such fine pictures, heavens! I cannot dare
   To turn my admiration, though unpossessed
   They be of what is worthy,—though not dressed
In lovely modesty, and virtues rare.
Yet these I leave as thoughtless as a lark;
   These lures I straight forget,—e'en ere I dine,

6

Or thrice my palate moisten: but when I mark
   Such charms with mild intelligences shine,
My ear is open like a greedy shark,
   To catch the tunings of a voice divine.

Ah! who can e'er forget so fair a being?
   Who can forget her half-retiring sweets?
   God! she is like a milk-white lamb that bleats
For man's protection. Surely the All-seeing,
Who joys to see us with His gifts agreeing,
   Will never give him pinions, who intreats
   Such innocence to ruin,—who vilely cheats
A dove-like bosom. In truth there is no freeing
One's thoughts from such a beauty; when I hear
   A lay that once I saw her hand awake,
Her form seems floating palpable, and near;
   Had I e'er seen her from an arbour take
A dewy flower, oft would that hand appear,
   And o'er my eyes the trembling moisture shake.

To {Mary Frogley}

Hadst thou lived in days of old,
O what wonders had been told
Of thy lively countenance,
And thy humid eyes that dance
In the midst of their own brightness,
In the very fane of lightness.
Over which thine eyebrows, leaning,
Picture out each lovely meaning:
In a dainty bend they lie,
Like to streaks across the sky,
Or the feathers from a crow,
Fallen on a bed of snow.
Of thy dark hair that extends
Into many graceful bends:
As the leaves of hellebore
Turn to whence they sprung before
And behind each ample curl
Peeps the richness of a pearl.
Downward too flows many a tress
With a glossy waviness;
Full, and round like globes that rise
From the censer to the skies
Through sunny air. Add too, the sweetness
Of thy honeyed voice; the neatness
Of thine ankle lightly turned:

With those beauties, scarce discerned,
Kept with such sweet privacy,
That they seldom meet the eye
Of the little loves that fly
Round about with eager pry.
Saving when, with freshening lave,
Thou dipp'st them in the taintless wave;
Like twin water-lilies, born
In the coolness of the morn.
O, if thou hadst breathèd then,
Now the Muses had been ten.
Couldst thou wish for lineage higher
Than twin sister of Thalia?
At least for ever, evermore,
Will I call the Graces four.

Hadst thou lived when chivalry
Lifted up her lance on high,
Tell me what thou wouldst have been?
Ah! I see the silver sheen
Of thy broidered, floating vest
Covering half thine ivory breast;
Which, Oh heavens! I should see,
But that cruel destiny
Has placed a golden cuirass there;
Keeping secret what is fair.
Like sunbeams in a cloudlet nested
Thy locks in knightly casque are rested:
O'er which bend four milky plumes
Like the gentle lily's blooms
Springing from a costly vase.
See with what a stately pace
Comes thine alabaster steed;
Servant of heroic deed!
O'er his loins, his trappings glow

Like the northern lights on snow.
Mount his back! thy sword unsheathe!
Sign of the enchanter's death;
Bane of every wicked spell;
Silencer of dragon's yell.
Alas! thou this wilt never do—
Thou art an enchantress too,
And wilt surely never spill
Blood of those whose eyes can kill.

To ———

Had I a man's fair form, then might my sighs
  Be echoed swiftly through that ivory shell
  Thine ear, and find thy gentle heart; so well
Would passion arm me for the enterprise:
But ah! I am no knight whose foeman dies;
  No cuirass glistens on my bosom's swell;
  I am no happy shepherd of the dell
Whose lips have trembled with a maiden's eyes.
Yet must I dote upon thee—call thee sweet,
  Sweeter by far than Hybla's honeyed roses
    When steeped in dew rich to intoxication.
Ah! I will taste that dew, for me 'tis meet,
  And when the moon her pallid face discloses,
    I'll gather some by spells, and incantation.

To a Young Lady who sent me a Laurel Crown

Fresh morning gusts have blown away all fear
   From my glad bosom: now from gloominess
   I mount for ever—not an atom less
Than the proud laurel shall content my bier.
No! by the eternal stars! or why sit here
   In the Sun's eye, and 'gainst my temples press
   Apollo's very leaves, woven to bless
By thy white fingers and thy spirit clear.
Lo! who dares say, "Do this"? Who dares call down
   My will from its high purpose? Who say, "Stand,"
Or "Go"? This very moment I would frown
   On abject Caesars—not the stoutest band
Of mailèd heroes should tear off my crown:
   Yet would I kneel and kiss thy gentle hand!

1860

Lines

Unfelt, unheard, unseen,
I've left my little queen,
Her languid arms in silver slumber lying:
    Ah! through their nestling touch,
    Who—who could tell how much
There is for madness—cruel, or complying?

    Those faery lids how sleek!
    Those lips how moist!—they speak,
In ripest quiet, shadows of sweet sounds:
    Into my fancy's ear
    Melting a burden dear,
How "Love doth know no fullness nor no bounds."

    True!—tender monitors!
    I bend unto your laws:
This sweetest day for dalliance was born!
    So, without more ado,
    I'll feel my heaven anew,
For all the blushing of the hasty morn.

Stanzas

I

You say you love; but with a voice
  Chaster than a nun's, who singeth
The soft Vespers to herself
  While the chime-bell ringeth—
    O love me truly!

II

You say you love; but with a smile
  Cold as sunrise in September,
As you were Saint Cupid's nun,
  And kept his weeks of Ember.
    O love me truly!

III

You say you love—but then your lips
  Coral tinted teach no blisses
More than coral in the sea—
  They never pout for kisses—
    O love me truly!

IV

You say you love; but then your hand
　　No soft squeeze for squeeze returneth,
It is like a statue's, dead—
　　While mine for passion burneth—
　　　　O love me truly!

V

O breathe a word or two of fire!
　　Smile, as if those words should burn me,
Squeeze as lovers should—O kiss
　　And in thy heart inurn me!
　　　　O love me truly!

"Hither, hither, love—"

Hither, hither, love—
　'Tis a shady mead—
Hither, hither, love,
　Let us feed and feed!

Hither, hither, sweet—
　'Tis a cowslip bed—
Hither, hither, sweet!
　'Tis with dew bespread!

Hither, hither, dear—
　By the breath of life—
Hither, hither, dear!
　Be the summer's wife!

Though one moment's pleasure
　In one moment flies,
Though the passion's treasure
　In one moment dies;

Yet it has not passed—
　Think how near, how near!—
And while it doth last,
　Think how dear, how dear!

Isabella and the Pot of Basil by William Holman Hunt.

Hither, hither, hither,
  Love this boon has sent—
If I die and wither
  I shall die content.

"Think not of it, sweet one, so—"

Think not of it, sweet one, so—
  Give it not a tear;
Sigh thou mayst, and bid it go
  Any, any where.

Do not look so sad, sweet one—
  Sad and fadingly;
Shed one drop, then it is gone,
  O 'twas born to die.

Still so pale? then, dearest, weep—
  Weep, I'll count the tears,
And each one shall be a bliss
  For thee in after years.

Brighter has it left thine eyes
  Than a sunny rill;
And thy whispering melodies
  Are tenderer still.

Yet—as all things mourn awhile
  At fleeting blisses,
E'en let us too! but be our dirge
  A dirge of kisses.

"In drear-nighted December"

I

In drear-nighted December,
     Too happy, happy tree,
Thy branches ne'er remember
     Their green felicity:
  The north cannot undo them,
  With a sleety whistle through them,
  Nor frozen thawings glue them
     From budding at the prime.

II

In drear-nighted December,
     Too happy, happy brook,
Thy bubblings ne'er remember
     Apollo's summer look;
But with a sweet forgetting,
They stay their crystal fretting,
Never, never petting
     About the frozen time.

III

Ah! would 'twere so with many
    A gentle girl and boy!
But were there ever any
    Writhed not of passèd joy?
  The feel of not to feel it,
  When there is none to heal it,
  Nor numbèd sense to steel it,
    Was never said in rhyme.

"When I have fears that I may cease to be"

When I have fears that I may cease to be
   Before my pen has gleaned my teeming brain,
Before high-pilèd books, in charactery,
   Hold like rich garners the full-ripened grain;
When I behold, upon the night's starred face,
   Huge cloudy symbols of a high romance,
And think that I may never live to trace
   Their shadows, with the magic hand of chance;
And when I feel, fair creature of an hour!
   That I shall never look upon thee more,
Never have relish in the faery power
   Of unreflecting love!—then on the shore
Of the wide world I stand alone, and think
Till love and fame to nothingness do sink.

"Oh blush not so! O blush not so!"

I

O blush not so! O blush not so!
  Or I shall think you knowing;
And if you smile the blushing while,
  Then maidenheads are going.

II

There's a blush for won't, and a blush for shan't,
  And a blush for having done it:
There's a blush for thought, and a blush for naught,
  And a blush for just begun it.

III

O sigh not so! O sigh not so!
  For it sounds of Eve's sweet pippin;
By those loosened hips you have tasted the pips
  And fought in an amorous nipping.

IV

Will you play once more at nice-cut-core,
  For it only will last our youth out?
And we have the prime of the kissing time,
  We have not one sweet tooth out.

V

There's a sigh for yes, and a sigh for no,
  And a sigh for I can't bear it!
O what can be done, shall we stay or run?
  O, cut the sweet apple and share it!

To ———

Time's sea hath been five years at its slow ebb,
   Long hours have to and fro let creep the sand,
Since I was tangled in the beauty's web,
   And snared by the ungloving of thy hand.
And yet I never look on midnight sky,
   But I behold thine eyes' well memoried light;
I cannot look upon the rose's dye,
   But to thy cheek my soul doth take its flight;
I cannot look on any budding flower,
   But my fond ear, in fancy at thy lips,
And hearkening for a love-sound, doth devour
   Its sweets in the wrong sense:—Thou dost eclipse
Every delight with sweet remembering,
And grief unto my darling joys dost bring.

"Where be ye going, you Devon maid?"

I

Where be ye going, you Devon maid?
  And what have ye there i' the basket?
Ye tight little fairy, just fresh from the dairy,
  Will ye give me some cream if I ask it?

II

I love your meads, and I love your flowers,
  And I love your junkets mainly,
But 'hind the door I love kissing more,
  O look not so disdainly.

III

I love your hills, and I love your dales,
  And I love your flocks a-bleating—
But O, on the heather to lie together,
  With both our hearts a-beating!

IV

I'll put your basket all safe in a *nook*,
  And your shawl I hang up *on this willow*,
And we will sigh in the daisy's eye
  And kiss on a grass-green pillow.

"Over the hill and over the dale"

Over the hill and over the dale,
And over the bourn to Dawlish—
Where gingerbread wives have a scanty sale
And gingerbread nuts are smallish.

Rantipole Betty she ran down a hill
And kicked up her petticoats fairly.
Says I, "I'll be Jack if you will be Jill."
So she sat on the grass debonairly.

"Here's somebody coming, here's somebody coming!"
Says I, " 'Tis the wind at a parley."
So without any fuss, any hawing and humming,
She lay on the grass debonairly.

"Here's somebody here, and here's somebody *there*!"
Says I, "Hold your tongue, you young gipsy."
So she held her tongue and lay plump and fair,
And dead as a Venus tipsy.

O who wouldn't hie to Dawlish fair,
O who wouldn't stop in a meadow?
O [who] would not rumple the daisies there,
And make the wild fern for a bed do?

"And what is love? It is a doll dressed up"

And what is love? It is a doll dressed up
For idleness to cosset, nurse, and dandle;
A thing of soft misnomers, so divine
That silly youth doth think to make itself
Divine by loving, and so goes on
Yawning and doting a whole summer long,
Till Miss's comb is made a pearl tiara,
And common Wellingtons turn Romeo boots;
Till Cleopatra lives at Number Seven,
And Antony resides in Brunswick Square.
Fools! if some passions high have warmed the world,
If queens and soldiers have played deep for hearts,
It is no reason why such agonies
Should be more common than the growth of weeds.
Fools! make me whole again that weighty pearl
The queen of Egypt melted, and I'll say
That ye may love in spite of beaver hats.

Song

I

Hush, hush! tread softly! hush, hush my dear!
All the house is asleep, but we know very well
That the jealous, the jealous old bald-pate may hear,
  Though you've padded his night-cap—O sweet Isabel!
    Though your feet are more light than a faery's feet,
    Who dances on bubbles where brooklets meet—
Hush, hush! tread softly! hush, hush my dear!
For less than a nothing the jealous can hear.

II

No leaf doth tremble, no ripple is there
  On the river—all's still, and the night's sleepy eye
Closes up, and forgets all its Lethean care,
  Charmed to death by the drone of the humming mayfly;
    And the moon, whether prudish or complaisant,
    Hath fled to her bower, well knowing I want
No light in the darkness, no torch in the gloom,
But my Isabel's eyes, and her lips pulped with bloom.

III

Lift the latch! ah gently! ah tenderly—sweet!
We are dead if that latchet gives one little clink!
Well done—now those lips, and a flowery seat—
The old man may dream, and the planets may wink;
The shut rose may dream of our loves, and awake
Full-blown, and such warmth for the morning take,
The stock-dove shall hatch her soft brace and shall coo,
While I kiss to the melody, aching all through!

The Eve of St. Agnes

I

St. Agnes' Eve—Ah, bitter chill it was!
The owl, for all his feathers, was a-cold;
The hare limped trembling through the frozen grass,
And silent was the flock in woolly fold:
Numb were the Beadsman's fingers, while he told
His rosary, and while his frosted breath,
Like pious incense from a censer old,
Seemed taking flight for heaven, without a death,
Past the sweet Virgin's picture, while his prayer he saith.

II

His prayer he saith, this patient, holy man;
Then takes his lamp, and riseth from his knees,
And back returneth, meagre, barefoot, wan,
Along the chapel aisle by slow degrees:
The sculptured dead, on each side, seem to freeze,
Emprisoned in black, purgatorial rails;
Knights, ladies, praying in dumb orat'ries,
He passeth by; and his weak spirit fails
To think how they may ache in icy hoods and mails.

III

    Northward he turneth through a little door,
    And scarce three steps, ere Music's golden tongue
    Flattered to tears this agèd man and poor;
    But no—already had his deathbell rung:
    The joys of all his life were said and sung:
    His was harsh penance on St. Agnes' Eve.
    Another way he went, and soon among
    Rough ashes sat he for his soul's reprieve,
And all night kept awake, for sinners' sake to grieve.

IV

    That ancient Beadsman heard the prelude soft;
    And so it chanced, for many a door was wide,
    From hurry to and fro. Soon, up aloft,
    The silver, snarling trumpets 'gan to chide:
    The level chambers, ready with their pride,
    Were glowing to receive a thousand guests:
    The carvèd angels, ever eager-eyed,
    Stared, where upon their heads the cornice rests,
With hair blown back, and wings put cross-wise on their breasts.

V

    At length burst in the argent revelry,
    With plume, tiara, and all rich array,
    Numerous as shadows haunting faerily
    The brain, new-stuffed, in youth, with triumphs gay
    Of old romance. These let us wish away,
    And turn, sole-thoughted, to one Lady there,
    Whose heart had brooded, all that wintry day,
    On love, and winged St. Agnes' saintly care,
As she had heard old dames full many times declare.

VI

    They told her how, upon St. Agnes' Eve,
    Young virgins might have visions of delight,
    And soft adorings from their loves receive
    Upon the honeyed middle of the night,
    If ceremonies due they did aright;
    As, supperless to bed they must retire,
    And couch supine their beauties, lily white;
    Nor look behind, nor sideways, but require
Of Heaven with upward eyes for all that they desire.

VII

    Full of this whim was thoughtful Madeline:
    The music, yearning like a God in pain,
    She scarcely heard: her maiden eyes divine,
    Fixed on the floor, saw many a sweeping train
    Pass by—she heeded not at all: in vain
    Came many a tip-toe, amorous cavalier,
    And back retired—not cooled by high disdain,
    But she saw not: her heart was otherwhere.
She sighed for Agnes' dreams, the sweetest of the year.

VIII

    She danced along with vague, regardless eyes,
    Anxious her lips, her breathing quick and short:
    The hallowed hour was near at hand: she sighs
    Amid the timbrels, and the thronged resort
    Of whisperers in anger, or in sport;
    'Mid looks of love, defiance, hate, and scorn,
    Hoodwinked with faery fancy—all amort,
    Save to St. Agnes and her lambs unshorn,
And all the bliss to be before to-morrow morn.

IX

 So, purposing each moment to retire,
 She lingered still. Meantime, across the moors,
 Had come young Porphyro, with heart on fire
 For Madeline. Beside the portal doors,
 Buttressed from moonlight, stands he, and implores
 All saints to give him sight of Madeline
 But for one moment in the tedious hours,
 That he might gaze and worship all unseen;
Perchance speak, kneel, touch, kiss—in sooth such things have been.

X

 He ventures in—let no buzzed whisper tell,
 All eyes be muffled, or a hundred swords
 Will storm his heart, Love's fev'rous citadel:
 For him, those chambers held barbarian hordes,
 Hyena foemen, and hot-blooded lords,
 Whose very dogs would execrations howl
 Against his lineage: not one breast affords
 Him any mercy, in that mansion foul,
Save one old beldame, weak in body and in soul.

XI

 Ah, happy chance! the agèd creature came,
 Shuffling along with ivory-headed wand,
 To where he stood, hid from the torch's flame,
 Behind a broad hall-pillar, far beyond
 The sound of merriment and chorus bland:
 He startled her; but soon she knew his face,
 And grasped his fingers in her palsied hand,
 Saying, "Mercy, Porphyro! hie thee from this place:
They are all here to-night, the whole blood-thirsty race!

XII

"Get hence! get hence! there's dwarfish Hildebrand—
He had a fever late, and in the fit
He cursèd thee and thine, both house and land:
Then there's that old Lord Maurice, not a whit
More tame for his grey hairs—Alas me! flit!
Flit like a ghost away." "Ah, gossip dear,
We're safe enough; here in this arm-chair sit,
And tell me how—" "Good Saints! not here, not here;
Follow me, child, or else these stones will be thy bier."

XIII

He followed through a lowly archèd way,
Brushing the cobwebs with his lofty plume,
And as she muttered, "Well-a—well-a-day!"
He found him in a little moonlight room,
Pale, latticed, chill, and silent as a tomb.
"Now tell me where is Madeline," said he,
"O tell me, Angela, by the holy loom
Which none but secret sisterhood may see,
When they St. Agnes' wool are weaving piously."

"St. Agnes? Ah! it is St. Agnes' Eve—
Yet men will murder upon holy days:
Thou must hold water in a witch's sieve,
And be liege-lord of all the Elves and Fays,
To venture so: it fills me with amaze
To see thee, Porphyro!—St. Agnes' Eve!
God's help! my lady fair the conjuror plays
This very night. Good angels her deceive!
But let me laugh awhile, I've mickle time to grieve."

Feebly she laugheth in the languid moon,
While Porphyro upon her face doth look,
Like puzzled urchin on an agèd crone
Who keepeth closed a wondrous riddle-book,
As spectacled she sits in chimney nook.
But soon his eyes grew brilliant, when she told
His lady's purpose; and he scarce could brook
Tears, at the thought of those enchantments cold,
And Madeline asleep in lap of legends old.

XVI

Suddenly a thought came like a full-blown rose,
Flushing his brow, and in his painèd heart
Made purple riot; then doth he propose
A stratagem, that makes the beldame start:
"A cruel man and impious thou art:
Sweet lady, let her pray, and sleep, and dream
Alone with her good angels, far apart
From wicked men like thee. Go, go!—I deem
Thou canst not surely be the same that thou didst seem."

"I will not harm her, by all saints I swear,"
Quoth Porphyro: "O may I ne'er find grace
When my weak voice shall whisper its last prayer,
If one of her soft ringlets I displace,
Or look with ruffian passion in her face:
Good Angela, believe me by these tears,
Or I will, even in a moment's space,
Awake, with horrid shout, my foeman's ears,
And beard them, though they be more fanged than wolves and bears."

"Ah! why wilt thou affright a feeble soul?
A poor, weak, palsy-stricken, churchyard thing,
Whose passing-bell may ere the midnight toll;
Whose prayers for thee, each morn and evening,
Were never missed."—Thus plaining, doth she bring
A gentler speech from burning Porphyro,
So woeful, and of such deep sorrowing,
That Angela gives promise she will do
Whatever he shall wish, betide her weal or woe.

XIX

Which was, to lead him, in close secrecy,
Even to Madeline's chamber, and there hide
Him in a closet, of such privacy
That he might see her beauty unespied,
And win perhaps that night a peerless bride,
While legioned faeries paced the coverlet,
And pale enchantment held her sleepy-eyed.
Never on such a night have lovers met,
Since Merlin paid his Demon all the monstrous debt.

XX

"It shall be as thou wishest," said the Dame:
"All cates and dainties shall be storèd there
Quickly on this feast-night; by the tambour frame
Her own lute thou wilt see. No time to spare,
For I am slow and feeble, and scarce dare
On such a catering trust my dizzy head.
Wait here, my child, with patience; kneel in prayer
The while. Ah! thou must needs the lady wed,
Or may I never leave my grave among the dead."

XXI

So saying, she hobbled off with busy fear.
The lover's endless minutes slowly passed;
The dame returned, and whispered in his ear
To follow her; with agèd eyes aghast
From fright of dim espial. Safe at last,
Through many a dusky gallery, they gain
The maiden's chamber, silken, hushed, and chaste;
Where Porphyro took covert, pleased amain.
His poor guide hurried back with agues in her brain.

Her faltering hand upon the balustrade,
Old Angela was feeling for the stair,
When Madeline, St. Agnes' charmèd maid,
Rose, like a missioned spirit, unaware:
With silver taper's light, and pious care,
She turned, and down the agèd gossip led
To a safe level matting. Now prepare,
Young Porphyro, for gazing on that bed—
She comes, she comes again, like ring-dove frayed and fled.

XXIII

Out went the taper as she hurried in;
Its little smoke, in pallid moonshine, died:
She closed the door, she panted, all akin
To spirits of the air, and visions wide—
No uttered syllable, or, woe betide!
But to her heart, her heart was voluble,
Paining with eloquence her balmy side;
As though a tongueless nightingale should swell
Her throat in vain, and die, heart-stiflèd, in her dell.

XXIV

A casement high and triple-arched there was,
All garlanded with carven imag'ries
Of fruits, and flowers, and bunches of knot-grass,
And diamonded with panes of quaint device,
Innumerable of stains and splendid dyes,
As are the tiger-moth's deep-damasked wings;
And in the midst, 'mong thousand heraldries,
And twilight saints, and dim emblazonings,
A shielded scutcheon blushed with blood of queens and kings.

XXV

Full on this casement shone the wintry moon,
And threw warm gules on Madeline's fair breast,
As down she knelt for heaven's grace and boon;
Rose-bloom fell on her hands, together pressed,
And on her silver cross soft amethyst,
And on her hair a glory, like a saint:
She seemed a splendid angel, newly dressed,
Save wings, for Heaven—Porphyro grew faint;
She knelt, so pure a thing, so free from mortal taint.

XXVI

Anon his heart revives; her vespers done,
Of all its wreathèd pearls her hair she frees;
Unclasps her warmèd jewels one by one;
Loosens her fragrant bodice; by degrees
Her rich attire creeps rustling to her knees:
Half-hidden, like a mermaid in sea-weed,
Pensive awhile she dreams awake, and sees,
In fancy, fair St. Agnes in her bed,
But dares not look behind, or all the charm is fled.

Soon, trembling in her soft and chilly nest,
In sort of wakeful swoon, perplexed she lay,
Until the poppied warmth of sleep oppressed
Her soothèd limbs, and soul fatigued away—
Flown, like a thought, until the morrow-day;
Blissfully havened both from joy and pain;
Clasped like a missal where swart Paynims pray;
Blinded alike from sunshine and from rain,
As though a rose should shut, and be a bud again.

XXVIII

Stolen to this paradise, and so entranced,
Porphyro gazed upon her empty dress,
And listened to her breathing, if it chanced
To wake into a slumbrous tenderness;
Which when he heard, that minute did he bless,
And breathed himself: then from the closet crept,
Noiseless as fear in a wide wilderness,
And over the hushed carpet, silent, stepped,
And 'tween the curtains peeped, where, lo!—how fast she slept.

Then by the bed-side, where the faded moon
Made a dim, silver twilight, soft he set
A table, and, half anguished, threw thereon
A cloth of woven crimson, gold, and jet—
O for some drowsy Morphean amulet!
The boisterous, midnight, festive clarion,
The kettle-drum, and far-heard clarinet,
Affray his ears, though but in dying tone;
The hall door shuts again, and all the noise is gone.

XXX

And still she slept an azure-lidded sleep,
In blanchèd linen, smooth, and lavendered,
While he from forth the closet brought a heap
Of candied apple, quince, and plum, and gourd,
With jellies soother than the creamy curd,
And lucent syrups, tinct with cinnamon;
Manna and dates, in argosy transferred
From Fez; and spicèd dainties, every one,
From silken Samarkand to cedared Lebanon.

XXXI

These delicates he heaped with glowing hand
On golden dishes and in baskets bright
Of wreathèd silver; sumptuous they stand
In the retirèd quiet of the night,
Filling the chilly room with perfume light.
"And now, my love, my seraph fair, awake!
Thou art my heaven, and I thine eremite:
Open thine eyes, for meek St. Agnes' sake,
Or I shall drowse beside thee, so my soul doth ache."

XXXII

Thus whispering, his warm, unnervèd arm
Sank in her pillow. Shaded was her dream
By the dusk curtains—'twas a midnight charm
Impossible to melt as iced stream:
The lustrous salvers in the moonlight gleam;
Broad golden fringe upon the carpet lies.
It seemed he never, never could redeem
From such a steadfast spell his lady's eyes;
So mused awhile, entoiled in woofèd fantasies.

Awakening up, he took her hollow lute,
Tumultuous, and, in chords that tenderest be,
He played an ancient ditty, long since mute,
In Provence called, "La belle dame sans mercy,"
Close to her ear touching the melody—
Wherewith disturbed, she uttered a soft moan:
He ceased—she panted quick—and suddenly
Her blue affrayèd eyes wide open shone.
Upon his knees he sank, pale as smooth-sculptured stone.

XXXIV

Her eyes were open, but she still beheld,
Now wide awake, the vision of her sleep—
There was a painful change, that nigh expelled
The blisses of her dream so pure and deep.
At which fair Madeline began to weep,
And moan forth witless words with many a sigh,
While still her gaze on Porphyro would keep;
Who knelt, with joinèd hands and piteous eye,
Fearing to move or speak, she looked so dreamingly.

XXXV

"Ah, Porphyro!" said she, "but even now
Thy voice was at sweet tremble in mine ear,
Made tuneable with every sweetest vow,
And those sad eyes were spiritual and clear:
How changed thou art! How pallid, chill, and drear!
Give me that voice again, my Porphyro,
Those looks immortal, those complainings dear!
O leave me not in this eternal woe,
For if thou diest, my Love, I know not where to go."

Beyond a mortal man impassioned far
At these voluptuous accents, he arose,
Ethereal, flushed, and like a throbbing star
Seen mid the sapphire heaven's deep repose;
Into her dream he melted, as the rose
Blendeth its odour with the violet—
Solution sweet. Meantime the frost-wind blows
Like Love's alarum pattering the sharp sleet
Against the window-panes; St. Agnes' moon hath set.

'Tis dark: quick pattereth the flaw-blown sleet.
"This is no dream, my bride, my Madeline!"
'Tis dark: the icèd gusts still rave and beat.
"No dream, alas! alas! and woe is mine!
Porphyro will leave me here to fade and pine.—
Cruel! what traitor could thee hither bring?
I curse not, for my heart is lost in thine,
Though thou forsakest a deceivèd thing—
A dove forlorn and lost with sick unprunèd wing."

"My Madeline! sweet dreamer! lovely bride!
Say, may I be for aye thy vassal blessed?
Thy beauty's shield, heart-shaped and vermeil dyed?
Ah, silver shrine, here will I take my rest
After so many hours of toil and quest,
A famished pilgrim—saved by miracle.
Though I have found, I will not rob thy nest
Saving of thy sweet self; if thou think'st well
To trust, fair Madeline, to no rude infidel.

XXXIX

    Hark! 'tis an elfin-storm from faery land,
    Of haggard seeming, but a boon indeed:
    Arise—arise! the morning is at hand.
    The bloated wassaillers will never heed—
    Let us away, my love, with happy speed—
    There are no ears to hear, or eyes to see,
    Drowned all in Rhenish and the sleepy mead;
    Awake! arise! my love, and fearless be,
For o'er the southern moors I have a home for thee."

XL

    She hurried at his words, beset with fears,
    For there were sleeping dragons all around,
    At glaring watch, perhaps, with ready spears—
    Down the wide stairs a darkling way they found.
    In all the house was heard no human sound.
    A chain-drooped lamp was flickering by each door;
    The arras, rich with horseman, hawk, and hound,
    Fluttered in the besieging wind's uproar;
And the long carpets rose along the gusty floor.

XLI

They glide, like phantoms, into the wide hall;
Like phantoms, to the iron porch, they glide;
Where lay the Porter, in uneasy sprawl,
With a huge empty flaggon by his side:
The wakeful bloodhound rose, and shook his hide,
But his sagacious eye an inmate owns.
By one, and one, the bolts full easy slide—
The chains lie silent on the footworn stones—
The key turns, and the door upon its hinges groans.

XLII

And they are gone—ay, ages long ago
These lovers fled away into the storm.
That night the Baron dreamt of many a woe,
And all his warrior-guests, with shade and form
Of witch, and demon, and large coffin-worm,
Were long be-nightmared. Angela the old
Died palsy-twitched, with meagre face deform;
The Beadsman, after thousand aves told,
For aye unsought for slept among his ashes cold.

C. Grignion sculp.

La Belle Dame sans Merci. A Ballad

I

O what can ail thee, knight-at-arms,
   Alone and palely loitering?
The sedge has withered from the lake,
   And no birds sing.

II

O what can ail thee, knight-at-arms,
   So haggard and so woe-begone?
The squirrel's granary is full,
   And the harvest's done.

III

I see a lily on thy brow,
   With anguish moist and fever-dew,
And on thy cheeks a fading rose
   Fast withereth too.

IV

I met a lady in the meads,
   Full beautiful—a faery's child,
Her hair was long, her foot was light,
   And her eyes were wild.

V

I made a garland for her head,
  And bracelets too, and fragrant zone;
She looked at me as she did love,
  And made sweet moan.

VI

I set her on my pacing steed,
  And nothing else saw all day long,
For sidelong would she bend, and sing
  A faery's song.

VII

She found me roots of relish sweet,
  And honey wild, and manna-dew,
And sure in language strange she said—
  "I love thee true."

VIII

She took me to her elfin grot,
  And there she wept and sighed full sore,
And there I shut her wild wild eyes
  With kisses four.

And there she lullèd me asleep
   And there I dreamed—Ah! woe betide!—
The latest dream I ever dreamt
   On the cold hill side.

I saw pale kings and princes too,
   Pale warriors, death-pale were they all;
They cried—"La Belle Dame sans Merci
   Thee hath in thrall!"

I saw their starved lips in the gloam,
   With horrid warning gapèd wide,
And I awoke and found me here,
   On the cold hill's side.

And this is why I sojourn here
   Alone and palely loitering,
Though the sedge is withered from the lake,
   And no birds sing.

"The day is gone, and all its sweets are gone!"

The day is gone, and all its sweets are gone!
   Sweet voice, sweet lips, soft hand, and softer breast,
Warm breath, light whisper, tender semi-tone,
   Bright eyes, accomplished shape, and languorous waist!
Faded the flower and all its budded charms,
   Faded the sight of beauty from my eyes,
Faded the shape of beauty from my arms,
   Faded the voice, warmth, whiteness, paradise—
Vanished unseasonably at shut of eve,
   When the dusk holiday—or holinight—
Of fragrant-curtained love begins to weave
   The woof of darkness thick, for hid delight;
But, as I've read love's missal through today,
He'll let me sleep, seeing I fast and pray.

Piazza di Spagna, Rome. Keats and Joseph Severn shared the apartment
on the third floor in the building at the right.
Keats's room was on the corner.

"What can I do to drive away"

What can I do to drive away
Remembrance from my eyes? for they have seen,
Ay, an hour ago, my brilliant Queen!
Touch has a memory. O say, love, say,
What can I do to kill it and be free
In my old liberty?
When every fair one that I saw was fair,
Enough to catch me in but half a snare,
Not keep me there;
When, howe'er poor or parti-coloured things,
My muse had wings,
And ever ready was to take her course
Whither I bent her force,
Unintellectual, yet divine to me—
Divine, I say! What sea-bird o'er the sea
Is a philosopher the while he goes
Winging along where the great water throes?

How shall I do
To get anew
Those moulted feathers, and so mount once more
Above, above
The reach of fluttering Love,
And make him cower lowly while I soar?
Shall I gulp wine? No, that is vulgarism,

A heresy and schism,
   Foisted into the canon law of love;
No—wine is only sweet to happy men;
   More dismal cares
   Seize on me unawares—
Where shall I learn to get my peace again?
To banish thoughts of that most hateful land,
Dungeoner of my friends, that wicked strand
Where they were wrecked and live a weckèd life;
That monstrous region, whose dull rivers pour,
Ever from their sordid urns into the shore,
Unowned of any weedy-hairèd gods;
Whose winds, all zephyrless, hold scourging rods,
Iced in the great lakes, to afflict mankind;
Whose rank-grown forests, frosted, black, and blind,
Would fright a Dryad; whose harsh-herbaged meads
Make lean and lank the starved ox while he feeds;
There flowers have no scent, birds no sweet song,
And great unerring Nature once seems wrong.

O, for some sunny spell
To dissipate the shadows of this hell!
Say they are gone—with the new dawning light
Steps forth my lady bright!
O, let me once more rest
My soul upon that dazzling breast!
Let once again these aching arms be placed,
The tender gaolers of thy waist!
And let me feel that warm breath here and there
To spread a rapture in my very hair—
O, the sweetness of the pain!
Give me those lips again!
Enough! Enough! It is enough for me
To dream of thee!

"I cry your mercy, pity, love—ay, love!"

I cry your mercy, pity, love—ay, love!
  Merciful love that tantalizes not,
One-thoughted, never-wandering, guileless love,
  Unmasked, and being seen—without a blot!
O! let me have thee whole,—all, all, be mine!
  That shape, that fairness, that sweet minor zest
Of love, your kiss—those hands, those eyes divine,
  That warm, white, lucent, million-pleasured breast—
Yourself—your soul—in pity give me all,
  Withhold no atom's atom or I die;
Or living on perhaps, your wretched thrall,
  Forget, in the mist of idle misery,
Life's purposes—the palate of my mind
Losing its gust, and my ambition blind!

"Bright star! would I were steadfast as thou art—"

Bright star! would I were steadfast as thou art—
   Not in lone splendour hung aloft the night
And watching, with eternal lids apart,
   Like nature's patient, sleepless Eremite,
The moving waters at their priestlike task
   Of pure ablution round earth's human shores,
Or gazing on the new soft-fallen mask
   Of snow upon the mountains and the moors—
No—yet still steadfast, still unchangeable,
   Pillowed upon my fair love's ripening breast,
To feel for ever its soft swell and fall,
   Awake for ever in a sweet unrest,
Still, still to hear her tender-taken breath,
And so live ever—or else swoon to death.

Fanny Brawne, from a miniature painted in 1833, twelve years after Keats's death.

To Fanny

I

Physician Nature! let my spirit blood!
  O ease my heart of verse and let me rest;
Throw me upon thy tripod till the flood
  Of stifling numbers ebbs from my full breast.
A theme! a theme! Great Nature! give a theme;
  Let me begin my dream.
I come—I see thee, as thou standest there,
Beckon me out into the wintry air.

II

Ah! dearest love, sweet home of all my fears,
  And hopes, and joys, and panting miseries,
Tonight, if I may guess, thy beauty wears
    A smile of such delight,
    As brilliant and as bright,
  As when with ravished, aching, vassal eyes,
    Lost in a soft amaze,
    I gaze, I gaze!

III

Who now, with greedy looks, eats up my feast?
   What stare outfaces now my silver moon!
Ah! keep that hand unravished at the least;
      Let, let, the amorous burn—
      But, prithee, do not turn
   The current of your heart from me so soon.
      O save, in charity,
      The quickest pulse for me!

IV

Save it for me, sweet love! though music breathe
      Voluptuous visions into the warm air,
Though swimming through the dance's dangerous wreath,
      Be like an April day,
      Smiling and cold and gay,
   A temperate lily, temperate as fair;
      Then, Heaven! there will be
      A warmer June for me.

V

Why, this—you'll say, my Fanny!—is not true:
   Put your soft hand upon your snowy side;
Where the heart beats; confess—'tis nothing new—
      Must not a woman be
      A feather on the sea,
   Swayed to and fro by every wind and tide?
      Of as uncertain speed
      As blow-ball from the mead?

VI

I know it—and to know it is despair
   To one who loves you as I love, sweet Fanny!

Deathbed sketch of Keats by Joseph Severn.

Whose heart goes fluttering for you everywhere,
    Nor, when away you roam,
    Dare keep its wretched home.
  Love, Love alone, has pains severe and many:
    Then, loveliest! keep me free
    From torturing jealousy.

VII

Ah! if you prize my subdued soul above
  The poor, the fading, brief, pride of an hour,
Let none profane my Holy See of Love,
    Or with a rude hand break
    The sacramental cake;
  Let none else touch the just new-budded flower;
    If not—may my eyes close,
    Love! on their last repose.